MW01175060

Choice of Market Proxy in the Capital Asset Pricing Model

Jason Chang

Choice of Market Proxy in the Capital Asset Pricing Model

A Closer Examination of Relative Risk in the CAPM

LAP LAMBERT Academic Publishing

Impressum/Imprint (nur für Deutschland/only for Germany)
Bibliografische Information der Deutschen Nationalbibliothek: Die Deutsche Nationalbibliothek verzeichnet diese Publikation in der Deutschen Nationalbibliografie; detaillierte bibliografische Daten sind im Internet über http://dnb.d-nb.de abrufbar.
Alle in diesem Buch genannten Marken und Produktnamen unterliegen warenzeichen-, marken- oder patentrechtlichem Schutz bzw. sind Warenzeichen oder eingetragene Warenzeichen der jeweiligen Inhaber. Die Wiedergabe von Marken, Produktnamen, Gebrauchsnamen, Handelsnamen, Warenbezeichnungen u.s.w. in diesem Werk berechtigt auch ohne besondere Kennzeichnung nicht zu der Annahme, dass solche Namen im Sinne der Warenzeichen- und Markenschutzgesetzgebung als frei zu betrachten wären und daher von jedermann benutzt werden dürften.

Coverbild: www.ingimage.com

Verlag: LAP LAMBERT Academic Publishing GmbH & Co. KG
Heinrich-Böcking-Str. 6-8, 66121 Saarbrücken, Deutschland
Telefon +49 681 3720-310, Telefax +49 681 3720-3109
Email: info@lap-publishing.com

Herstellung in Deutschland:
Schaltungsdienst Lange o.H.G., Berlin
Books on Demand GmbH, Norderstedt
Reha GmbH, Saarbrücken
Amazon Distribution GmbH, Leipzig
ISBN: 978-3-8465-4996-4

Imprint (only for USA, GB)
Bibliographic information published by the Deutsche Nationalbibliothek: The Deutsche Nationalbibliothek lists this publication in the Deutsche Nationalbibliografie; detailed bibliographic data are available in the Internet at http://dnb.d-nb.de.
Any brand names and product names mentioned in this book are subject to trademark, brand or patent protection and are trademarks or registered trademarks of their respective holders. The use of brand names, product names, common names, trade names, product descriptions etc. even without a particular marking in this works is in no way to be construed to mean that such names may be regarded as unrestricted in respect of trademark and brand protection legislation and could thus be used by anyone.

Cover image: www.ingimage.com

Publisher: LAP LAMBERT Academic Publishing GmbH & Co. KG
Heinrich-Böcking-Str. 6-8, 66121 Saarbrücken, Germany
Phone +49 681 3720-310, Fax +49 681 3720-3109
Email: info@lap-publishing.com

Printed in the U.S.A.
Printed in the U.K. by (see last page)
ISBN: 978-3-8465-4996-4

ABSTRACT

One of the most popular and widely accepted financial valuation models is the Capital Asset Pricing Model (CAPM). This model intuitively takes relative risk into pricing a financial asset. Since Sharpe first developed the CAPM in 1964, the return on the Standard and Poor's 500 (S&P 500) market index has been used as the proxy for the market return. This proxy has not been updated to reflect the globalization of finance and the growth of global stock markets relative to domestic markets. The market proxy is one of the most important factors if not the most important factor in measuring relative risk. This thesis examines a potentially more appropriate global index, the Standard and Poor's Global 1200. Although the S&P 500 captures globalization to a certain extent due to the global nature of the domestic companies included in the index, the S&P Global 1200 index is a broader global index and may now be more suitable given the increased globalization the world economy has experienced in recent decades.

A byproduct of this thesis is the finding that beta, a measure of relative volatility of an individual stock or a portfolio of stocks relative to the broader market broke

i

down during the 2008 financial crisis. Further study is needed to examine whether beta breakdown in all extreme financial crisis and therefore cannot be used as an investment filtering tool during harsh financial environments.

TABLE OF CONTENTS

LIST OF TABLES

LIST OF FIGURES

LIST OF ABBREVIATIONS

APT	Arbitrage Pricing Theory
ASX	Australian Securities Exchange
CAPM	Capital Asset Pricing Model
CBOE	Chicago Board Options Exchange
CDS	Credit Default Swaps
DCF	Discounted Cash Flow
ESS	Explained Sum of Squares
ETF	Exchange-Traded Fund
GDP	Gross Domestic Product
ICAPM	Intertemporal Capital Asset Pricing Model
IMF	International Monetary Fund
IXJ	iShares Standard and Poor's Global Healthcare Sector Index Fund
IXN	iShares Standard and Poor's Global Technology Sector Index Fund
IXP	iShares Standard and Poor's Global Telecommunications Sector Index Fund
MPT	Modern Portfolio Theory
NASDAQ	National Association of Securities Dealers Automated Quotation System
NYSE	New York Stock Exchange
OLS	Ordinary least Squares
OPM	Option Pricing Model
RSS	Residual Sum of Squares
S&P	Standard and Poor's
SCA	Sales Comparison Approach
TOPIX	Tokyo Stock Price Index
TSE	Tokyo Stock Exchange
TSS	Total Sum of Squares
TSX	Stock of Exchange of Toronto
U.S.	United States

CHAPTER I

Introduction

Price and risk are two factors that any investors would consider prior to purchasing a financial asset. The Capital Asset Pricing Model (CAPM) is the most widely known valuation model that attempts to find an equilibrium point between risk and return for financial assets. The CAPM prices an asset from the investor's perspective and intuitively takes risk (relative to the market's volatility) into consideration when deriving the expected return of an asset or investment.

In general, the most interesting and difficult business question is measuring financial asset values. Today, businesses commonly value assets with methods like 1) valuation based on cash flows, 2) relative value (also known as sales comparison approach), and 3) option pricing. Valuation utilizing cash flow to price an asset (also known as the Discounted Cash Flow (DCF) model) uses future free cash flow projections and discounts them (often using the weighted average cost of capital) to arrive at a present value (Ross, Westerfield and Jordan 2003).

1

The relative valuation model (also known as the sales comparison approach (SCA)) is more commonly used in real estate appraisal. The SCA is a simple valuation model but it is also constrained by market sales data; for many new creative financial products, such as credit default swaps (CDSs) based on subprime mortgages[1], this approach would be limited by its lack of market and historic sales transactions.

For creative financial products such as options, the Black-Scholes Option Pricing Model (OPM) is the more appropriate approach. An option is a contract that gives the buyer the right (but not the obligation) to buy or sell a specific financial product, officially known as the option's underlying instrument or underlying asset. For equity options, the underlying instrument is a stock, an exchange-traded fund (ETF), or a similar product. The contract itself is very precise. It establishes a specific price, called the strike price, at which the contract may be exercised, or acted on. And it has an expiration date. When an option expires, it no longer has value and no

---

[1] During the 1990s, subprime lenders had revenues of $30 billion dollars annually. In 2000, there had been $130 billion in subprime mortgage lending, and $55 billion worth of those loans had been repackaged as mortgage bonds. In 2005 there would be $625 billion in subprime mortgage loans and $507 billion of which found its way into mortgage bonds (Lewis 2010).

longer exists (The Options Industry Council 2011). The
Black-Scholes model develops partial differential equations
whose solution is widely used in the pricing of European-
style options[2]. This model, based on the formula and
empirical tests, shows that the transactional costs of
options pricing will cause a systematic misestimation of
value and "does not imply profit opportunities for a
speculator in the option market" (Black and Scholes 1973).
Simply put: option buyers pay prices that are consistently
higher than those estimated by the formula. In contrast,
option writers receive prices that are similar to the level
predicted by the formula. There are large transaction
costs in the option market, all of which are paid by option
buyers. Thus, speculative buyers experience losses on
average. This situation provides more evidence of
disequilibrium between risk and price within financial
markets.

The CAPM embodies factors from the three foregoing
approaches of valuation. Since the DCF model takes past
cash flow transactions and projects them into the future as
expected cash flow, then discounts these to the current
period to derive its present value, this is a

---

[2] An "American option" is one that can be exercised at any time up to
the date the option expires. A "European option" is one that can be
exercised only on a specified future date (Black and Scholes 1973).

characteristic shared by the CAPM; expectation of future returns based on past returns.

The relative valuation approach takes similar products in the market and categorizes them to derive an expected price for assets that share similar characteristics. Logically, this approach measures a price based on past sales transactions within similar markets and it assumes that the risks borne by the asset are relative to the market's performance in this category. The CAPM has a parallel approach to measuring risk (systematic risk[3]); it regresses an asset's past performance to the market's return and assigns a specific measurement of risk to each asset, known as beta.

Table 1: *Total Risk = Systematic Risk + Unsystematic Risk*

Systematic Risk:	Unsystematic Risk:
Undiversifiable	Diversifiable
Market risk	Firm-specific
	Idiosyncratic

Source: (Berk and DeMarzo 2011)

The last approach, the Black-Scholes Option Pricing Model (OPM), shares similar assumptions with the CAPM, such

---

[3] Every financial investment is exposed to risk. We can further break down risk into two categories: Total Risk equals to systematic risk (undiversifiable) plus unsystematic risk (diversifiable). Systematic risk is the risk inherent to the entire market or entire market segment. Unsystematic risk is firm-specific risk that is inherent in each investment, which can be reduced through appropriate diversification.

as there are no transaction costs in buying or selling the stock or the option. This common feature of the OPM and the CAPM attempts to simplify reality and avoid minor frictions created by financial regulations, therefore, obtaining the true behavior of an ideal efficient market valuation.

History of CAPM

The first portfolio valuation concept was developed by Harry Markowitz (1952)[4], and was named the Modern Portfolio Theory (MPT). In Markowitz's model, a portfolio is selected by an investor at time $t - 1$ that produces a stochastic return at time t. The basic assumptions of the model are: investors are risk averse and, when selecting among portfolios, the only relevance is the mean and variance of the investor's one-period return on the portfolio. As a result, investors will select "mean-variance-efficient" portfolios, implying that the portfolios: 1) minimize the variance of portfolio return, given the anticipated or expected return, and 2) maximize expected return, given variance (Fama and French 2004). Markowitz's approach established a mean-variance framework for portfolio selection (Markowitz 1952). Building on this

---

[4] Harry Markowitz: The Markowitz Model is the first model to deal explicitly with risk in a portfolio.

model: Sharpe (1964)[5] and Lintner (1965)[6] developed the Capital Asset Pricing Model (CAPM) which introduced a new definition of asset risk. From this perspective, each financial asset's risk is viewed by how it performs with the market as a whole, instead of its individual volatility. The CAPM was also very successful and the first apparent model to show how to assess the risk of the cash flow from an investment opportunity and to estimate a project's cost of capital, the expected rate of return those investors will demand from the project. The relationship between anticipated risk and expected return described by the CAPM has profoundly influenced economists understanding of how capital markets work.

During the 1970s and 1980s, the CAPM was modified and further developed by other economists into two main directions: the Intertemporal Capital Asset Pricing Model (ICAPM), and the Arbitrage Pricing Theory (APT). The ICAPM showed that systematic risk is no longer the only derivation of market portfolio, but also by a vector of

---

[5] William F. Sharpe, The Professor of Operations Research, University of Washington; published "Capital Asset Prices: A theory of market Equilibrium under Conditions of Risk" at The Journal of Finance September 1964. This paper is recognized as one of the foundation for CAPM.
[6] John Linter is considered one of the founders of CAPM. The publication of "The valuation of Risk Assets and The Selection of Risky Investments in Stock Portfolios and Capital Budgets" The Review of Economics and Statistics February 1965, Linter introduced a new definition of asset risk.

other state variables. In contrast, the APT repositions expected returns against a set of exogenous factors rather than one factor - the market portfolio or consumption. Unsystematic risk (undiversified risk) is therefore influenced by a number of factors and not just the market portfolio or consumption.

Since the development of the CAPM in the 1960s, this pricing approach has gone through rigorous examination and been increasingly used among the financial industry. Most studies has found that a positive and significant relationship between the ex post mean return and the corresponding risk index (beta). The positive significance have enhanced the role of CAPM and in fact, beta (systematic or undiversifiable risk), is reported by numerous institutional investors' services such as Value Line, Standard and Poor's, and Merrill Lynch. However, a test performed by Fama and French in 1992 did not find such a positive relationship. The test involves comprehensive empirical analysis of common stocks covering the period 1963 to 1990, concluding that beta has no explanatory power and "the relation between beta and average return is much flatter than the Sharpe-Lintner CAPM predicts" (Fama and French 2004). According to this study, the returns on the low beta portfolios are higher than expected; in contrast, the returns on the high beta portfolios are lower than anticipated[7]. Thus, the CAPM's validity was seriously challenged. In response, Fischer Black[8] points out that Fama and French cannot prove wrong the hypothesis that the slope line between beta and average return is positive in the time period of the study. Moreover, if the slope is truly zero, it implies dramatic investment opportunities for investors who use beta to filter and price assets. A person who normally holds both stocks and bonds or stocks and cash can reallocate the portfolio of similar total risk but higher expected return by emphasizing low-beta stocks[9]. Furthermore, Sharpe thinks that the finding of Fama and French do not contradict conventional view of the CAPM. Simply put: the concern is future, as opposed to historical, investment return[10].

Another interesting critique of the CAPM mention by Fama and French is the market proxy problem; the argument is that the market portfolio at the heart of the CAPM is

[7] Fama and French provided examples such as the predicted return on the portfolio with the lowest beta is 8.3% per year; the actual return is 11.1%. The predicted return on the portfolio with the highest beta is 16.8% per year; the actual return is 13.7% (Fama and French 2004).
[8] Fischer Black was an American economist, best known as one of the authors of the famous Black-Scholes Option Pricing Model.
[9] See Fischer Black "Beta and Return" the Journal of Portfolio Management Fall 1993 Page 9
[10] See Haim Levy "Risk and Return: An Experiment Analysis" International Economic Review vol. 38, No., 1, February 1997

theoretically and empirically elusive (Roll 1977). It is theoretically unclear which assets (for example, human capital, real estate, and etc…) can legitimately be excluded from the market portfolio, and inaccessible data substantially limits the assets that are included. As a result, tests of the CAPM are forced to use proxies for the market portfolio, in effect questioning if the proxies are on the minimum variance frontier. Roll[11] argues that the tests of the CAPM use market proxies, not the true comprehensive market portfolio, and therefore nothing can be concluded about the CAPM.

Traditional application of the CAPM tends to use Standard and Poor's 500 index as a default proxy for the market. But the S&P 500 is not the only market proxy that can be utilized; other options such as the S&P 400, the Dow Jones Industrial Average, and the Wilshire 5000 are among the choices. However, there are problems with each index, but the worst problem is one that affects all indexes, as Roll (1977) pointed out: because all indexes are just samples of the real market for all risky assets, it is difficult and impossible, to know which index is an adequate proxy for the unknown world.

---

[11] Richard Roll is an American economist, best known for his work on portfolio theory and asset pricing, both theoretical and empirical.

Another common problem is that the U.S. equity market represents a large portion of each index. With the merger of financial markets around the world, such as the New York Stock Exchange's possible merger with Germany's premier stock market (Lucchetti 2011), there is no doubt that the world's financial markets are becoming more easily accessible by common investors. This trend shows that S&P 500 as the default proxy for market portfolio is becoming dated and inadequate; the solution would be to select a more appropriate index that reflects the trend of globalization and represents financial markets around the world with the correct ratio in the index's composition.

The purpose of this thesis is to examine whether a better alternative of market proxy to the traditional choice, the S&P 500, exists. The intention is to select a market proxy that includes global markets around the world such as the S&P Global 1200, therefore sampling a more comprehensive market proxy for the application of the CAPM.

CHAPTER II

Market Proxy

The Standard and Poor's 500 is a free-float
capitalization-weighted index, and remains the most widely
regarded best single gauge of the large cap U.S. equities
market since its inception in 1957. The index has over US$
4.83 trillion benchmarked, with index assets comprising
approximately US$ 1.1 trillion of this total. The index
includes five hundred leading companies in the foremost
industries of the U.S. economy, capturing 75% coverage of
U.S. equities (Standard & Poor's Financial Services LLC
2011).

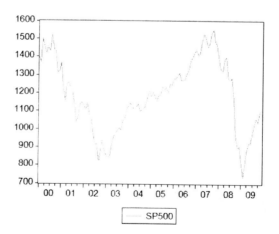

Figure 1: S&P 500 (Jan. 2000 to Dec. 2009)
Data Source: (Yahoo! Finance 2011)

The S&P 500 index focuses on U.S. based companies, although there are a few legacy companies with headquarters in other nations. In general, any new company added to the index is U.S. based, and, when an S&P 500 company shifts its headquarter overseas, it is replaced by a U.S. company[12]. Because of this basic strategy of U.S. centric selection coupled with changes in the international economic balance, the S&P 500 is no longer an adequate market proxy for the CAPM. According to the International Monetary Fund (IMF), in 2010 the United States now ranks as the second largest economy in terms of nominal GDP at approximately US$ 14.62 trillion, having been dethroned by the European Union with a nominal GDP of US$ 16.10 trillion (total global nominal GDP is around US$ 62 trillion). This means that U.S. GDP now represents less than 25% of the global total. In view of these changes, the other portion of global GDP should be represented if the market proxy is to retain validity.

---

[12] When Transocean's headquarter relocated from Houston to Switzerland in 2008, it was delisted from the S&P 500 and replaced by Equitable Resources Inc. (Godt 2008)

Table 2: *Countries by Nominal GDP*

Country	Nominal GDP (trillions US$)
European Union[13]	16.10
United States	14.62
China	5.74
Japan	5.39
Brazil	2.02
Canada	1.56

Data Source: (International Monetary Fund n.d.)

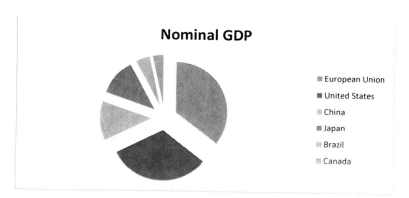

Figure 2: Countries' Nominal GDP
Data Source: (International Monetary Fund n.d.)

Globalization is a process by which regional
economies, societies, and cultures have become integrated

---

[13] The European Union (EU) is an economic and political union of 27
member states that are located primarily in Europe.

through communication, transportation, and trade. With the advent of technology and the breaking down of trade barriers, economic globalization is happening at a faster pace than most have expected. Financial markets (such as NYSE, NASDEQ, CBOE, TSE, and etc…) around the world allow the common investor to freely move resources, causing movement of capitals towards higher returns.

A U.S. centric market proxy is no longer an accurate reflection of the market portfolio that the theoretic Capital Asset Pricing Model (CAPM) pursues. Reflecting the already significant and accelerating globalization of business, it is clear that today in order to be effective, a market proxy can no longer restrict itself to evaluating companies in the U.S., but must integrate economies outside America in its calculations. In view of these considerations, this thesis intends to show that the Standard and Poor's Global 1200 is a more suitable alternative as the market proxy for the application of the CAPM than the S&P 500.

The S&P Global 1200 is a composite of 31 local markets and approximately 70% of the world's capital markets. The index is a composite of seven headline indices: S&P 500 (United States), S&P Europe 350, S&P TOPIX 150 (Japan),

14

S&P/TSX 60 (Canada), S&P/ASX AII Australian 50, S&P Asia 50
(Hong Kong, Korea, Singapore, Taiwan), and S&P Latin
America 40 (Mexico, Brazil, Peru, Chile) (S&P Global 1200
2011). The combination of multiple local markets into
seven regional indices allows common investors to achieve
the level of global exposure and makes the S&P Global 1200
the best measure of the worldwide investable market and
hence, an more appropriate market proxy.

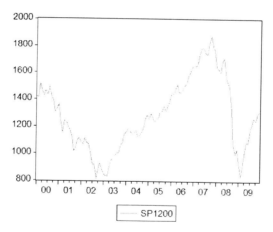

Figure 3: S&P Global 1200 (Jan. 2000 to Dec. 2009)
Data Source: (Bloomberg Terminal 2010)

Beta

The relative volatility of returns can be defined as 'beta', also known as systematic risk, under this concept: if the asset's returns tend to move up and down more dramatically than do the overall market's returns, then the asset is considered relatively more volatile – more risky – and it will have a higher beta (Harrington 1987). Beta is the only asset-specific or portfolio-specific factor in the CAPM that also links the investor's expectations of returns from the asset or portfolio with his or her expectations of returns from the market. Under the CAPM, beta has relevant influences on the calculation of expected return therefore the estimation of beta must be accurate.

Mathematically, beta is defined as:

$$\beta_j = \frac{covariance\ (R_j,\ R_m)}{variance\ (R_m)}$$

Where:

$variance(R_m)$ = the uncertainty attached to economic events

$covariance(R_j,R_m)$ = the responsiveness of an asset's rate of return(R_j) to those things that also change the market's rate of return(R_m)

j = an asset, stock, or portfolio

m = the market

16

The mathematical expression of beta is fairly straight forward, but each variable is based on expectations. The most difficult issue regarding estimation of beta is due to the result of compromises – 1) using sample variances and covariance (which may change over time) in place of population parameters (fixed over time); and 2) utilizing inadequate proxies for expectation factors such as "the market". The most common proxy has been the historic returns of the asset in relation to that of a broad-based index of common stock returns (market portfolio). Using an index that represents only a portion of the stock market is a compromise and when the traditional market proxy, the S&P 500, is outdated relative to globalization, then it should be replaced.

Estimating Using Regression Technique

The relationship between the return of the asset relative to the market can be examined simply by plotting the relationship over time. At any given time, the return from the asset and that from the market are represented by a dot on the graph (figure 4). To utilize this information, we can fit a line to the data using regression technique. This line is called the security characteristic line and the relationship can be explained by using the basic geometric formula for a line $(y = \alpha + \beta x)$.

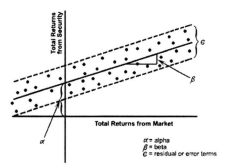

Figure 4: Security Characteristic Line

The basic concept behind regression analysis is the methodology of ordinary least squares, OLS, which minimizes the squared errors of each data point from the fitted line.

The intercept or α is the return from the asset if the
return from the market were zero[14]. The slope or β is the
incremental return expected from the asset or portfolio as
the market return becomes higher or lower.

Using basic regression technique, estimating beta (β)
from historic data, a simple version of the formula for a
straight line is utilized, known as the 'market model' and
it is presented as follow:

$$R_{jt} = \alpha_j + \beta_j R_{mt} + \epsilon_j$$

Where:

R = total returns

j = a firm or portfolio

t = the time period

m = the market

α = alpha or intercept; the return from the asset when the
return of the market was zero

β = the systematic risk or beta, the slope of the line

ϵ = the residuals or errors of the fitted line (assumed to
be normally distributed)

The strong similarity between the market model and the
CAPM is extremely confusing, but rest assured, both models

---

[14] This condition only happens when total returns from the asset and the
market are considered. If the excess returns, that are asset's return
minus the risk free rate and market's return minus the risk free rate,
were plotted then the line would have gone through the origin and the
alpha would have been zero.

are not the same. The CAPM is inherently constrained by assumptions while the market model is freely estimated by generating a linear relationship between the returns from the asset and the returns from the market. The only assumption that the market model makes is that history is an accurate predictor of the future. This assumption is not generally true, but this is not an issue of central concern in this study. To continue on with identifying a more appropriate market proxy, the traditional method of estimating beta will be implemented and the assumption of past performance being an accurate predictor of the future expectation will be temporarily regarded as true for the purpose of this thesis.

CHAPTER III

Regression Analysis

The first step to determine if the Standard and Poor's Global 1200 index is more appropriate than the Standard and Poor's 500 index as the market proxy for the Capital Asset Pricing Model (CAPM) is to derive the market's rate of return. This can be done with the index level data that was obtained earlier. The formula to determine the rate of return is set forth as:

$$Rate\ of\ return_{market} = 100 * Log\ (\ \frac{Market\ index\ level\ (t)}{Market\ index\ level\ (t-1)}\ )$$

Where:

t = time

After processing the data, this thesis will assume normal distribution of the rate of return for both the S&P 500 and the S&P Global 1200.

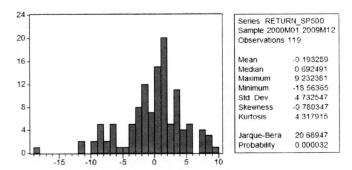

Series RETURN_SP500	
Sample 2000M01 2009M12	
Observations 119	
Mean	-0.193289
Median	0.692491
Maximum	9.232381
Minimum	-18.56365
Std. Dev.	4.732547
Skewness	-0.780347
Kurtosis	4.317915
Jarque-Bera	20.68947
Probability	0.000032

Figure 5: S&P 500's rate of return (histogram)

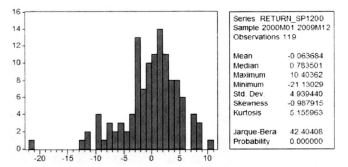

Series RETURN_SP1200	
Sample 2000M01 2009M12	
Observations 119	
Mean	-0.063684
Median	0.783501
Maximum	10.40362
Minimum	-21.13029
Std. Dev.	4.939440
Skewness	-0.987915
Kurtosis	5.155963
Jarque-Bera	42.40408
Probability	0.000000

Figure 6: S&P Global 1200's rate of return (histogram)

From the S&P 500 and the S&P Global 1200 histograms, a
visual inspection suggests both market's rate of return may
be normally distributed. To continue on with evaluating if
the S&P Global 1200 is more suitable than the S&P 500 as a
market proxy, sample assets and betas will be needed to
test the outcomes.

22

Since the objective of this thesis is to examine the more appropriate market proxy, the stability of beta must be considered. Individual securities' beta tends to be unstable overtime due to the influence of management or unsystematic risk. The portfolio beta, as expected, is quite stable. The stability is the result of the individual securities' negative correlation with other stocks in the same diversified portfolio, showing that beta estimation errors canceled each other out. For this very reason, the beta estimation of this study will be based on portfolio betas.

Sample Portfolios

Exchange Traded Funds (ETFs) are relatively new financial products. They are investment funds traded on securities exchanges, similar to stocks. This characteristic permits the market to determine a real-time price close to the net asset value of ETFs. An ETF holds assets such as stocks, commodities, or bonds. ETFs are structured like index mutual funds, resulting in a diversified portfolio of securities that may track specific indices. Taking advantage of ETFs features, a selection of different ETFs will act as different sample portfolios in the verification of market proxy in this thesis.

23

As of May 2010, Blackrock's iShares is the world's largest ETF provider with more than 440 ETFs globally totaling approximately $480 billion in asset (iShares n.d.). To verify the results of this thesis, three ETFs will be selected and act as three separate sample portfolios. The returns of each ETF will be obtained directly from iShares' corporate website, this data in turn being used to regress against the market proxy and ultimately obtain each ETF's beta. The three ETFs selected to act as sample portfolios are: 1) iShares S&P Global Healthcare Sector Index Fund (IXJ), 2) iShares S&P Global Technology Sector Index Fund (IXN), and 3) iShares S&P Global Telecommunications Sector Index Fund (IXP). The selection process was random and the only restriction for each ETF is that it must have been publicly traded for longer than 6 years; this requirement is a must to obtain statistic relevance.

iShares S&P Global Healthcare Sector

The iShares S&P Global Healthcare Sector Index Fund (IXJ) seeks investment results that correspond generally to the price and yield performance, before fees and expenses, of companies that Standard & Poor's deems part of the healthcare sector of the economy and important to global markets, as represented by the S&P Global Healthcare Sector Index (iShares 2011).

Table 3: *IXJ Top Daily Holdings*

Top Daily Holdings* as of 4/19/2011	View all holdings
JOHNSON&JOHNSON	7.78%
PFIZER INC	7.45%
NOVARTIS AG-REG	7.20%
GLAXOSMITHKLINE PLC	4.77%
ROCHE HOLDING AG-GENUSSCHEIN	4.73%
MERCK&CO. INC	4.72%
SANOFI-AVENTIS	3.65%
ABBOTT LABORATORIES	3.59%
ASTRAZENECA PLC	3.05%
BAYER AG	2.90%
Total	49.84%

holdings are subject to change

Data Source: (iShares 2011)

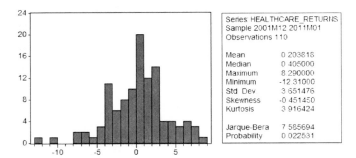

Figure 7: IXJ rate of return (histogram)

The S&P Global Health Care Sector Index Fund's histogram visually suggests the assumption of normal returns may be appropriate. The data also shows a range of returns between -12.31 to 8.29 and a mean of 0.204.

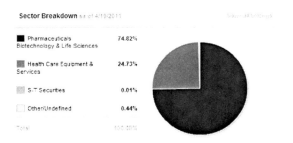

Figure 8: IXJ Sector Breakdown

Data Source: (iShares 2011)

iShares S&P Global Technology Sector Index Fund

The iShares S&P Global Technology Sector Index Fund (IXN) seeks investment results that correspond generally to the price and yield performance, before fees and expenses, of companies that Standard & Poor's deems part of the information technology sector of the economy and important to global markets, as represented by the Standard & Poor's Global Information Technology Sector Index (iShares 2011).

Table 4: *IXN Top Daily Holdings*

Top Daily Holdings* as of 4/8/2011	View all holdings
APPLE INC	10.59%
INTL BUSINESS MACHINES CORP	6.87%
MICROSOFT CORP	6.48%
GOOGLE INC-CL A	4.83%
ORACLE CORP	4.46%
SAMSUNG ELECTR-GDR REGS 144A	4.40%
INTEL CORP	3.63%
CISCO SYSTEMS INC	3.26%
QUALCOMM INC	2.96%
HEWLETT-PACKARD CO	2.92%
Total	50.39%

*Holdings are subject to change.

Data Source: (iShares 2011)

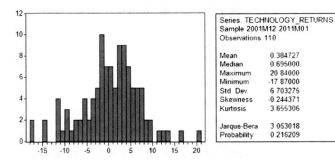

Figure 9: IXN rate of return (histogram)

The S&P Global Technology Sector Index Fund's histogram
visually suggests the assumption of normal returns may be
appropriate.   The data also shows a range of returns
between -17.87 to 20.84 and a mean of 0.385.

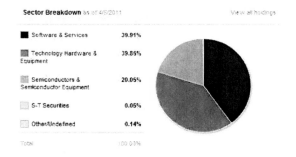

Figure 10: IXN Sector Breakdown
Data Source: (iShares 2011)

iShares S&P Global Telecommunications Sector Index Fund

The iShares S&P Global Telecommunications Sector Index Fund (IXP) seeks investment results that correspond generally to the price and yield performance, before fees and expenses, of companies that Standard & Poor's deems part of the telecommunications sector of the economy and important to global markets, as represented by the Standard & Poor's Global Telecommunications Sector Index (iShares 2011).

Table 5: *IXP Top Daily Holdings*

Top Daily Holdings* as of 4/5/2011	View all holdings
AT&T INC	15.05%
VODAFONE GROUP PLC	12.47%
VERIZON COMMUNICATIONS INC	8.92%
TELEFONICA SA	8.38%
CHINA MOBILE LTD	4.13%
DEUTSCHE TELEKOM AG-REG	4.03%
FRANCE TELECOM SA	3.72%
TELSTRA CORP LTD	2.77%
AMERICA MOVIL SAB DE CV-SER L	2.76%
NIPPON TELEGRAPH & TELEPHONE	2.71%
Total	64.93%

Data Source: (iShares 2011)

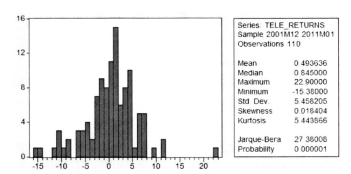

Figure 11: IXP rate of return (histogram)

The S&P Global Telecommunications Sector Index Fund's histogram visually suggests the assumption of normal returns may be appropriate. The data also shows a range of returns between -15.38 to 22.90 and a mean of 0.494.

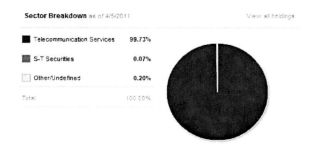

Figure 12: IXP Sector Breakdown

Data Source: (iShares 2011)

Measurement Period

To calculate beta, one must choose the data's length of time to include in the analysis. Determining the analytical time horizon is very important. Fundamentally, the measurement or holding period must be long enough to allow a statistically significant sample, but it must not be so long as to include information that does not reflect the relationships likely to persist into the future (Harrington 1987).

Alexander and Chervany (1980), studying beta stability, estimated the optimal interval over which to calculate a beta. Gathering data from 1950-67, the study found smaller absolute errors were associated with a six-year horizon, although it was insignificantly different from four years (Alexander and Chervany 1980). While results are subject to verification for different time periods and samples, many still believe, from a statistical perspective, that the longer the period, the better the data. This thesis intends to maintain a time horizon of data between four to six years for the simple fact of satisfying statistical minimal requirements and the avoidance of including unnecessary macro events such as the 2008 financial crisis.

Regression Results

Using Ordinary Least Squares (OLS) regression methodology, each ETF's rate of return is plotted against the market proxy's rate of return during the same time period. Since two market proxies are being evaluated, two independent regressions would need to be performed to obtain the proper beta results for each ETF portfolio:

Table 6: *Healthcare & S&P 500 regression*

Dependent Variable: HEALTHCARE_RETURNS
Method: Least Squares
Date: 04/07/11   Time: 11:43
Sample: 2002M01 2006M12
Included observations: 60

Variable	Coefficient	Std. Error	t-Statistic	Prob.
C	0.149610	0.253708	0.589692	0.5577
SP500	0.542302	0.070741	7.666024	0.0000

R-squared	0.503288	Mean dependent var	0.340500
Adjusted R-squared	0.494724	S.D. dependent var	2.751335
S.E. of regression	1.955724	Akaike info criterion	4.212163
Sum squared resid	221.8417	Schwarz criterion	4.281975
Log likelihood	-124.3649	F-statistic	58.76792
Durbin-Watson stat	2.269238	Prob(F-statistic)	0.000000

32

Table 7: *Healthcare & S&P Global 1200 regression*

Dependent Variable: HEALTHCARE_RETURNS
Method: Least Squares
Date: 04/07/11   Time: 11:44
Sample: 2002M01 2006M12
Included observations: 60

Variable	Coefficient	Std. Error	t-Statistic	Prob.
C	-0.001767	0.259155	-0.006820	0.9946
SP1200	0.526295	0.070097	7.508101	0.0000

R-squared	0.492881	Mean dependent var	0.340500
Adjusted R-squared	0.484138	S.D. dependent var	2.751335
S.E. of regression	1.976107	Akaike info criterion	4.232899
Sum squared resid	226.4898	Schwarz criterion	4.302711
Log likelihood	-124.9870	F-statistic	56.37158
Durbin-Watson stat	2.099572	Prob(F-statistic)	0.000000

Table 8: *Technology & S&P 500 regression*

Dependent Variable: TECHNOLOGY_RETURNS
Method: Least Squares
Date: 04/07/11   Time: 11:45
Sample: 2002M01 2006M12
Included observations: 60

Variable	Coefficient	Std. Error	t-Statistic	Prob.
C	-0.266266	0.372995	-0.713859	0.4782
SP500	1.706722	0.104002	16.41051	0.0000

R-squared	0.822795	Mean dependent var	0.334500
Adjusted R-squared	0.819740	S.D. dependent var	6.772160
S.E. of regression	2.875259	Akaike info criterion	4.982928
Sum squared resid	479.4926	Schwarz criterion	5.052739
Log likelihood	-147.4878	F-statistic	269.3049
Durbin-Watson stat	2.094531	Prob(F-statistic)	0.000000

Table 9: *Technology & S&P Global 1200 regression*

Dependent Variable: TECHNOLOGY_RETURNS
Method: Least Squares
Date: 04/07/11   Time: 11:46
Sample: 2002M01 2006M12
Included observations: 60

Variable	Coefficient	Std. Error	t-Statistic	Prob.
C	-0.691593	0.464440	-1.489091	0.1419
SP1200	1.577796	0.125623	12.55977	0.0000
R-squared	0.731168	Mean dependent var		0.334500
Adjusted R-squared	0.726532	S.D. dependent var		6.772160
S.E. of regression	3.541442	Akaike info criterion		5.399710
Sum squared resid	727.4249	Schwarz criterion		5.469521
Log likelihood	-159.9913	F-statistic		157.7477
Durbin-Watson stat	2.067020	Prob(F-statistic)		0.000000

Table 10: Telecommunications & S&P regression

Dependent Variable: TELE_RETURNS
Method: Least Squares
Date: 04/07/11   Time: 11:47
Sample: 2002M01 2006M12
Included observations: 60

Variable	Coefficient	Std. Error	t-Statistic	Prob.
C	0.162510	0.380705	0.426867	0.6711
SP500	1.360292	0.106152	12.81463	0.0000
R-squared	0.738991	Mean dependent var		0.641333
Adjusted R-squared	0.734491	S.D. dependent var		5.695382
S.E. of regression	2.934692	Akaike info criterion		5.023847
Sum squared resid	499.5202	Schwarz criterion		5.093659
Log likelihood	-148.7154	F-statistic		164.2147
Durbin-Watson stat	1.526197	Prob(F-statistic)		0.000000

34

Table 11: *Telecommunications & S&P Global 1200 regression*

Dependent Variable: TELE_RETURNS
Method: Least Squares
Date: 04/07/11   Time: 11:47
Sample: 2002M01 2006M12
Included observations: 60

Variable	Coefficient	Std. Error	t-Statistic	Prob.
C	-0.203103	0.412518	-0.492349	0.6243
SP1200	1.298467	0.111579	11.63719	0.0000

R-squared	0.700141	Mean dependent var		0.641333
Adjusted R-squared	0.694971	S.D. dependent var		5.695382
S.E. of regression	3.145527	Akaike info criterion		5.162605
Sum squared resid	573.8718	Schwarz criterion		5.232417
Log likelihood	-152.8782	F-statistic		135.4243
Durbin-Watson stat	1.526867	Prob(F-statistic)		0.000000

After performing regression analysis for each ETF portfolio using the S&P 500 and the S&P Global 1200 as market proxies, six beta results were obtained:

Table 12: *Beta Results (Jan. 2002 to Dec. 2006)*

	Healthcare	Technology	Telecom
S&P 500	0.542302	1.706722	1.360292
S&P 1200	0.526295	1.577796	1.298467

To answer the question of which market proxy is more appropriate for the application of CAPM, a re-examination of the S&P 500 regression versus the S&P Global 1200 regression will need to be done to statistically distinguish one result from another. But more importantly, can the statistical result be matched with the theoretical

35

conclusion that this thesis seeks? The exploration of this topic will continue in the next chapter of this study.

CHAPTER IV

S&P 500 versus S&P Global 1200

The basic concept of regression analysis is to estimate a linear relationship through many data points. Using this regression fitted line; a relationship can be observed between the independent and dependent variables. Using three sample ETF returns and plotting it against the Standard and Poor's 500 index and the Standard and Poor's Global 1200 index independently, two regressions were generated for each sample ETF portfolio. The problem on hand is to identify which regression, the S&P 500 versus the S&P Global 1200, has a better fitted line that describes a more accurate relationship.

There are regression summary statistics that can provide a useful measure of the fit between the estimated regression line and the data. The most common regression statistic that explains the relationship between variables is the explained sum of squares also known as R-squared or goodness of fit. A good regression equation is one which helps explain a large proportion of the variance of dependent variable or in this case, the returns of each sample portfolio. Large errors or residuals imply a poor fit; in contrast, small errors or residuals imply a good

37

fit. The problem with using the error or residual as a measure of goodness of fit is that its value depends on the units of the dependent variable. To resolve this issue that is unit-free, it seems plausible to use the residual variance divided by the variation of Y (dependent variable):

$$Variation\ (Y) = \sum (Y_i - \bar{Y})^2$$

The goal is to divide the variation of Y (dependent variable) into two components, that variation which can be explained by the regression and that which cannot:

$$\underset{\substack{Total\ Sum\ of\ Squares \\ (TSS)}}{\frac{\sum (Y_i - \bar{Y})^2}{}} = \underset{\substack{Explained\ Sum\ of \\ Squares\ (ESS)}}{\frac{\sum (\hat{Y}_i - \bar{Y})^2}{}} + \underset{\substack{Residual\ Sum\ of \\ Squares\ (RSS)}}{\frac{\sum e^2}{}}$$

To normalize the variation, both sides of the equation are divided by the total sum of square to arrive at:

$$1 = \frac{ESS}{TSS} + \frac{RSS}{TSS}$$

From this derivation, R-squared (R^2) of the regression equation can be defined as:

$$R^2 = 1 - \frac{RSS}{TSS} = \frac{ESS}{TSS}$$

R-squared is the proportion of the total variation in Y
(dependent variable) explained by the regression of Y
(dependent variable) on X (independent variable) (Pindyck
and Rubinfeld 1998). Understanding the concepts behind R-
squared, each regression's validity can be judged and
selected based on this criterion.

Table 13: *R-squared Summary*

	Healthcare	Technology	Telecom
S&P 500	0.503288	0.822795	0.738991
S&P 1200	0.492881	0.731168	0.700141

According to the R-squared summary (table 13), the
statistics indicate that the S&P 500's regression is
marginally superior at describing the relationship between
the portfolio's return and market's return versus the S&P
Global 1200 as the market proxy.

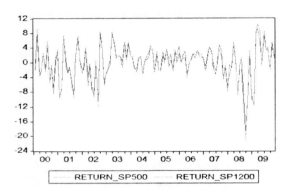

Figure 13: S&P 500 vs. S&P Global 1200 Returns

Why is that? There are many possibilities that can explain this outcome. One is that globalization's effect has not fully influenced the data set (January, 2002 to December, 2006) which is used in the regression analysis. The accelerating globalization effects will eventually influence the overall investable market and if one uses data sets from now and onward, one might find that the statistic outcome will match the theoretic predication more accurately. Secondly, the S&P Global 1200 is composed of the S&P 500 and other indices; thus both are highly correlated (figure 13) with each other and other indices has a marginally influence on the market's return as a whole in the last decade (opportunities in emerging markets only became more widely available in recent years), this

40

may also have weighted S&P 500 more favorably in the overall investable market.

Test of the CAPM

Another comparison that one can make to distinguish the S&P 500 versus the S&P Global 1200 is to use the beta generated by this study, forecast the following periodic monthly returns (January, 2007) and compare to the actual value. This was the original intention of the Capital Asset Pricing Model (CAPM), to forecast and value an investment; and it might have a more conclusive indication of which market proxy is more appropriate.

To test the outcome of the CAPM using the betas generated by this thesis, the risk free rate will be needed. The risk-free rate (R_f) is the least discussed of the three CAPM factors. Both in academic research and in practical applications of the CAPM, the 90-day Treasury bill rate has been virtually the only proxy used for the risk-free asset. This is based on the assumption that the United States will never default on its debt obligation, which using common and political logic, it can be assumed to be true for the foreseeable future.

The CAPM describes the relationship between expected return on an individual security or portfolio and the beta of the security or portfolio, and can be written as:

$$E(R_i) = R_f + \beta(E(R_m) - R_f)$$

Where,

R_i = Return of the individual security or portfolio

R_f = Risk-free rate

β = Individual security or portfolio beta

R_m = Return of the market

After obtaining the risk-free rate and using the beta generated by this study, the calculation can be done using the CAPM equation to estimate the expected return for the three sample portfolios. Since the betas were generated using monthly returns from 2002 to 2006, an estimation of January, 2007's return for all three sample portfolios will be performed and using the residual (error) variance, selection of which market proxy is more appropriate can be decided solely by this statistic:

Table 14: *CAPM Results (January, 2007)*

Sample Portfolio	Expected Return S&P 500	Expected Return S&P 1200	Actual Return	Absolute Value of Residual S&P 500	Absolute Value of Residual S&P 1200
Healthcare (IXJ)	0.95	0.72	0.77	0.18	0.05
Technology (IXN)	2.10	1.32	-0.34	2.44	1.66
Telecom (IXP)	1.75	1.16	4.03	2.28	2.87

According to CAPM calculations (table 14), the S&P Global 1200 as market proxy has smaller errors in calculating two out of three sample portfolio's expected returns. From this perspective, it would seem that the S&P Global 1200 is more than adequate as a replacement market proxy for the S&P 500. But is this really a solid conclusion? There are still many questions regarding the

43

CAPM that need to be resolved prior to obtaining a guaranteed result. But in the current time period, what can be concluded is that the S&P Global 1200 is an adequate replacement for the S&P 500 as a market proxy. At the very least, both indices are interchangeable as a market proxy for the CAPM. As globalization's effects accelerate and begin to influence the overall global investable market, the result might shift more favorably towards using the S&P Global 1200 as the default market proxy in the application of CAPM. Further study is needed to support this contention.

CHAPTER V

Beta during Crisis

As the late-2000s financial crisis appeared, the
volatility of the financial markets had a negative effect
on financial models such as the Capital Asset Pricing Model
(CAPM) and led to a breakdown of betas. The collapse of
the U.S. housing bubble, which peaked in 2006, caused the
values of securities tied to U.S. real estate pricing to
plummet, ultimately damaging financial institutions
globally. Questionable banking liquidity, declines in
credit availability, and damaged investor confidence had a
negative impact on global stock markets, where securities
suffered large losses during 2008 and early-2009.

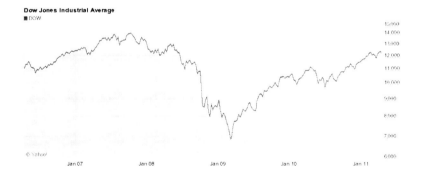

Figure 14: Dow Jones Average (2006 to 2012)

For example, the Dow Jones Industrial Average went from a high of 14,164 in October of 2007 to a low of 6,763 in March of 2009 (figure 20); this index gave back 52.2% of its value within 15 months (Polsson 2010).

What happened to beta during financial crisis? While processing regression analysis for this thesis, a byproduct of curiosity caused the inclusion of a data set during the financial meltdown. Using the same methodology of market model to generate betas, taking data of portfolio and market returns from November, 2006 to December, 2009 (38 observations): the result suggested a breakdown of beta and the CAPM.

Table 15: *Healthcare & S&P 500 regression (Crisis)*

Dependent Variable: HEALTHCARE
Method: Least Squares
Date: 04/18/11   Time: 15:36
Sample: 2006M11 2009M12
Included observations: 38

Variable	Coefficient	Std. Error	t-Statistic	Prob.
C	0.100320	0.749480	0.133853	0.8943
SP500	0.184877	0.130814	1.413289	0.1662
R-squared	0.052566	Mean dependent var		-0.005789
Adjusted R-squared	0.026249	S.D. dependent var		4.658409
S.E. of regression	4.596864	Akaike info criterion		5.939822
Sum squared resid	760.7217	Schwarz criterion		6.026010
Log likelihood	-110.8566	F-statistic		1.997386
Durbin-Watson stat	1.996618	Prob(F-statistic)		0.166160

Table 16: *Healthcare & S&P 1200 Global regression (Crisis)*

Dependent Variable: HEALTHCARE
Method: Least Squares
Date: 04/18/11   Time: 15:41
Sample: 2006M11 2009M12
Included observations: 38

Variable	Coefficient	Std. Error	t-Statistic	Prob.
C	0.064948	0.752098	0.086356	0.9317
SP1200	0.148593	0.118713	1.251693	0.2188

R-squared	0.041705	Mean dependent var	-0.005789
Adjusted R-squared	0.015086	S.D. dependent var	4.658409
S.E. of regression	4.623137	Akaike info criterion	5.951220
Sum squared resid	769.4422	Schwarz criterion	6.037409
Log likelihood	-111.0732	F-statistic	1.566736
Durbin-Watson stat	1.961655	Prob(F-statistic)	0.218754

Both regressions of Healthcare versus the S&P 500 and the S&P Global 1200 had estimated statistically insignificant betas. The R-squared statistic was also insignificant, a conclusion which would make the broader market insignificant with regards to the Healthcare sector.

Table 17: *Technology & S&P 500 regression (Crisis)*

Dependent Variable: TECH
Method: Least Squares
Date: 04/18/11   Time: 15:46
Sample: 2006M11 2009M12
Included observations: 38

Variable	Coefficient	Std. Error	t-Statistic	Prob.
C	0.471855	0.994598	0.474418	0.6381
SP500	0.482371	0.173596	2.778693	0.0086

R-squared	0.176600	Mean dependent var	0.195000
Adjusted R-squared	0.153727	S.D. dependent var	6.631228
S.E. of regression	6.100270	Akaike info criterion	6.505739
Sum squared resid	1339.679	Schwarz criterion	6.591928
Log likelihood	-121.6090	F-statistic	7.721136
Durbin-Watson stat	1.916226	Prob(F-statistic)	0.008618

47

Table 18: *Technology & S&P Global 1200 regression (Crisis)*

Dependent Variable: TECH
Method: Least Squares
Date: 04/18/11   Time: 15:55
Sample: 2006M11 2009M12
Included observations: 38

Variable	Coefficient	Std. Error	t-Statistic	Prob.
C	0.406332	0.988113	0.411221	0.6833
SP1200	0.443926	0.155966	2.846293	0.0073

R-squared	0.183699	Mean dependent var	0.195000
Adjusted R-squared	0.161024	S.D. dependent var	6.631228
S.E. of regression	6.073915	Akaike info criterion	6.497080
Sum squared resid	1328.128	Schwarz criterion	6.583268
Log likelihood	-121.4445	F-statistic	8.101382
Durbin-Watson stat	1.930549	Prob(F-statistic)	0.007258

Both regressions of Technology versus the S&P 500, and the S&P Global 1200 generated statistically significant betas, unfortunately the R-squared statistic is relatively low compared to earlier regressions, meaning movements in broader markets had far less correlation with movement in technology stocks than in the past. The betas also indicated that the portfolio of the technology sector went from high risk to low risk relative to market volatility. The data of both sets of regression overlapped, but had opposite conclusions regarding this sector of financial asset.

Table 19: *Telecommunications & S&P 500 regression (Crisis)*

Dependent Variable: TELECOM
Method: Least Squares
Date: 04/18/11   Time: 16:14
Sample: 2006M11 2009M12
Included observations: 38

Variable	Coefficient	Std. Error	t-Statistic	Prob.
C	0.591729	0.807265	0.733004	0.4683
SP500	0.395035	0.140899	2.803664	0.0081

R-squared	0.179217	Mean dependent var		0.365000
Adjusted R-squared	0.156417	S.D. dependent var		5.390809
S.E. of regression	4.951285	Akaike info criterion		6.088367
Sum squared resid	882.5479	Schwarz criterion		6.174556
Log likelihood	-113.6790	F-statistic		7.860531
Durbin-Watson stat	1.827001	Prob(F-statistic)		0.008090

Table 20: *Telecommunications & S&P Global 1200 regression (Crisis)*

Dependent Variable: TELECOM
Method: Least Squares
Date: 04/18/11   Time: 16:20
Sample: 2006M11 2009M12
Included observations: 38

Variable	Coefficient	Std. Error	t-Statistic	Prob.
C	0.542588	0.797064	0.680734	0.5004
SP1200	0.373043	0.125811	2.965110	0.0053

R-squared	0.196283	Mean dependent var		0.365000
Adjusted R-squared	0.173957	S.D. dependent var		5.390809
S.E. of regression	4.899539	Akaike info criterion		6.067355
Sum squared resid	864.1973	Schwarz criterion		6.153544
Log likelihood	-113.2797	F-statistic		8.791876
Durbin-Watson stat	1.908256	Prob(F-statistic)		0.005342

Both regressions from the Telecommunications versus the S&P 500 and the S&P Global 1200 had generated statistically significant betas, but also lower R-squared

statistic relative to earlier regressions.

Table 21: *Beta Results (Financial Crisis)*

	Healthcare	Technology	Telecom
S&P 500	0.185#	0.482	0.395
S&P 1200	0.149#	0.444	0.373

#statistically insignificant

> High beta or low, [Warren] Buffett is having none
> of it. "Beta is nice and mathematical," he says.
> "But it's wrong. It is not a measure of risk."
> Buffett then compares beta - as he frequently
> compares other investment concepts – to the price
> of farmland.
>
> "Take farmland here in Nebraska: the price of
> land went from $2,000 to $600 per acre. The beta
> of farms went way up, so according to standard
> economic theory, I was taking more risk buying at
> $600." He lets this sink in. "That's nonsense,"
> he says flatly. (Matthews 2009)

After examining regressions using data during the

financial meltdown, every single sector under study had

experienced less volatility relative to the market as a

whole. The purpose of beta was to identify which

individual security or portfolio was more or less volatile

than the market itself, therefore influencing the expected

return of the financial asset under the CAPM. But if the

market itself was more volatile than any financial assets, it rendered beta useless in pricing of any financial asset.

Conclusion

The CAPM is a simple and intuitive financial model for pricing a financial asset. The model measures an important factor of any investment decision, relative risk. There are obvious assumptions that are unrealistic, but these do not destroy the model's ability to describe or predict. There are some factors that limit the model, such as inflation, deflation, war and international involvement that may not be testable, but ultimately, the CAPM has been widely used by investment banks, investment analysts, and corporate financial officers.

Since Sharpe published the CAPM in 1964, a voluminous body of literature has been written based on this model. Although Fama and French (1992) made a persuasive case against the CAPM, recent studies have challenged this argument. Besides Fama and French's challenge, the model has not been updated to reflect the current economic trend towards globalization. As the general theory for a market proxy that it should encompass all investable market in the world: the conventional choice of the Standard and Poor's 500 is becoming outdated and the Standard and Poor's Global

1200 should be a more adequate replacement than any other available indices.

As shown in this thesis, the S&P 500 regressions had marginally superior R-squared statistic compared to the S&P Global 1200's regressions. Currently, the result does not clearly suggest a superior market proxy in the S&P Global 1200. But as globalization continues on, the support for the S&P 500 will begin to be limited by its exposure to U.S. centric financial markets. Using the estimated betas, the S&P Global 1200 had smaller error in forecasting future expected returns in two out of three sample portfolios. From this perspective, the S&P Global 1200 is more than adequate in replacing the S&P 500 as the default market proxy.

A byproduct of this thesis is the finding of beta breakdowns during the 2008 financial crisis. When the market as a whole is more volatile than any investable financial assets, then all betas would appear to be less than one and render beta useless as a filter for making investment decision. This also creates the possibility of the CAPM miscalculating the expected returns due to the fact of artificially low betas caused by the financial crisis, resulting in an inconclusive prediction of financial asset values.

The result of this study does show that during normal economic times there is general agreement with the CAPM that risk and return are found to be strongly associated. Anticipating further globalization, utilizing the proper market proxy such as the S&P Global 1200: the CAPM could still have something to offer and it can be modified to remain a useful filter for financial professionals making investment decisions.

REFERENCES

Alexander, Gordon J., and Norman L. Chervany. "On the Estimation and Stability of Beta." *Journal of Financial and Quantitative Analysis*, 1980: 123-137.

Berk, Jonathan, and Peter DeMarzo. *Corporate Finance.* Boston: Pearson Eduction, Inc, 2011.

Black, Fischer, and Myron Scholes. "The Pricing of Options and Corporate Liabilities." *The Journal of Political Economy*, 1973: 637-654.

Bloomberg Terminal. *S&P1200.* San Francisco State University, November 14, 2010.

Fama, Eugene F., and Kenneth R. French. "The Capital Asset Pricing Model: Theory and Evidence." *Journal of Economic Perspectives*, 2004: 25-46.

Godt, Nick. *Equitable Resources joins S&P 500, replaces Transocean: S&P.* December 12, 2008. http://www.marketwatch.com/story/equitable-resources-joins-sp-500-replaces-transocean-sp (accessed March 14, 2011).

Harrington, Diana R. *Modern Portfolio Theory, The Capital Asset Pricing Model & Arbitrage Pricing Theory: A User's Guide.* Englewood Cliffs: Prentice-Hall, Inc., 1987.

International Monetary Fund. www.imf.org (accessed March 14, 2011).

iShares. *Breadth and Depth of iShares ETFs.* http://us.ishares.com/understand_etf/why_ishares/modular.htm (accessed April 5, 2011).

—. *S&P Global Healtcare Sector Index Fund.* April 6, 2011. http://us.ishares.com/product_info/fund/overview/IXJ.htm (accessed April 6, 2011).

—. *S&P Global Technology Sector Index Fund.* April 6, 2011. http://us.ishares.com/product_info/fund/overview/IXN.htm (accessed April 6, 2011).

—. *S&P Global Telecommunications Sector Index Fund.* April
6, 2011.
http://us.ishares.com/product_info/fund/overview/IXP.h
tm (accessed April 6, 2011).

Lewis, Michael. *The Big Short.* New York: W.W. Norton &
Company, Inc., 2010.

Lucchetti, Aaron. "NYSE Takeover Faces Touchy Issues." *The
Wall Street Journal*, 2011.

Markowitz, Harry. "Portfolio Selection." *The Journal of
Finance*, 1952: 77-91.

Matthews, Jeff. *Pilgrimage to Warren Buffett's Omaha.* New
York: McGraw-Hill, 2009.

Pindyck, Robert S., and Daniel L. Rubinfeld. *Econometric
Models and Economic Forecasts.* Boston: McGraw-Hill,
1998.

Polsson, Ken. *Chronology of Dow Jones Industrial Average.*
July 1, 2010.
http://www.islandnet.com/~kpolsson/dowjones/dow1954.ht
m (accessed April 16, 2011).

Roll, Richard. "A Critique of the Asset Pricing Theory's
Tests' Part I: On Past and Potential Testability of
the Theory." *Journal of Financial Economics*, 1977:
129-176.

Ross, Stephen A., Randolph W. Westerfield, and Bradford D.
Jordan. *Fundamentals of Corporate Finance.* New York:
McGraw-Hill Higher Education, 2003.

"S&P Global 1200." *Standard and Poor's.* 2011.
http://www.standardandpoors.com/servlet/BlobServer?blo
bheadername3=MDT-
Type&blobcol=urldata&blobtable=MungoBlobs&blobheaderva
lue2=inline%3B+filename%3DFactsheet_SP_Global_1200.pdf
&blobheadername2=Content-
Disposition&blobheadervalue1=application%2Fpdf&blob
(accessed March 15, 2011).

Standard & Poor's Financial Services LLC. *S&P 500*. 2011.
    http://www.standardandpoors.com/indices/sp-
    500/en/us/?indexId=spusa-500-usduf--p-us-l-- (accessed
    March 14, 2011).

The Options Industry Council. *What is an Option?* 2011.
    http://www.optionseducation.org/basics/whatis/default.
    jsp (accessed February 16, 2011).

Yahoo! Finance. *S&P 500 INDEX*. 2011.
    http://finance.yahoo.com/q;_ylt=ArOHMwMDPZ7EB3PAOoZ07S
    G7YWsA;_ylu=X3oDMTFiZG1nMGV1BHBvcwM1BHN1YwNtYXJrZXRtdW
    1tYXJ5SW5kaWN1cwRzbGsDc2FtcHA1MDA-?s=^GSPC (accessed
    March 14, 2011).

CPSIA information can be obtained at www.ICGtesting.com
Printed in the USA
LVOW11s2321171115

463092LV00002B/158/P

9 783846 549964